25 Letters

25 Letters

Wade J. Savage

Library of Congress Control Number:		2010902050
ISBN:	Hardcover	978-1-4500-4332-8
	Softcover	978-1-4500-4331-1
	Ebook	978-1-4500-4333-5

Every good and perfect gift is from above, and cometh down from the Father of lights, whom is no variableness, neither shadow of turning.

James 1:17

December 2008

All bible quotes are from—New American Standard Bible: Reference Edition: Collins Publishers

This book was printed in the United States of America.

To order additional copies of this book, contact:
Xlibris Corporation
1-888-795-4274
www.Xlibris.com
Orders@Xlibris.com
69784

In dedication to my Family:

Andrea, Cory, Penny, Colin, Christian and Cornelius

Without you I would not have made it this far, I love you all with all of my heart.

My Shiloh AME Church family: You are the best, thank you Rev. Charlotte Clemons for being there for my family

FOREWORD

THE YEAR 2008 has been a most difficult year for me. You see I lost my job and I lost the ability to provide for my family. I, however, was not the only person put in this terrible situation. The recession of 2008 into 2009 has been relentless in its ability to destroy lives and make the weak of faith do horrific things to their families and to themselves.

I never imaged that I would be in this situation. But, then again, we cannot fully understand the ways of our Maker. And if you feel that you do not have a Maker, then you can never truly understand the desires of your heart. We all think we control our own destiny. Why not? We wake up every morning with a plan. A schedule. Things we want to do and need to do. But; stop, look and listen to the "things" that happen to you everyday and you quickly find that what you planned, scheduled and hoped for do not materialize as planned.

Let me begin by laying down some foundation. I grew up in a household full of boys, six boys to be exact. I was the next to the youngest. I was the smallest. I was the most ill-tempered. Consequently, I was the one with the least amount of confidence. Not a good combination to say the least. An example of this is the fact that when I ran away from home at the age of eleven, I did not make it far. My place of freedom was the roof of the house. It did not take them long to find me. The whole neighborhood could see me. Not the best idea I have ever had. Unfortunately, it was also not the worst.

I, however, had wonderful parents who let all of us be ourselves, no matter what that self turned out to be. My mother worked for the Social Security Administration and my father worked for the United States Postal Service. That is where my trouble began it seems. You see both parents went to work everyday. I cannot remember them not going to work, except for when they had to come up to my school because I had gotten into trouble again. Again having a temper, big mouth, and little body is not a receipt for success. But, I must say, it does sound like the making of a good postal manager.

Having good parents to most people would be a blessing and it is a blessing. But what children do not see is that working all the time and being a good provider has its drawbacks, if not properly explained and demonstrated. I did not know the difficultly of maintaining family and work in its proper balance once I grew up. The lesson I wished I had learned from their hard work is that being a provider means more then just providing money. Anyone can give money, but the strong and mighty also can give love and support while being the very best at their job. This is tricky, but very rewarding.

Fast forward to 2008. I had reached the level of Postmaster in the United States Postal Service. My parents were proud of my accomplishment, as were my brothers. Four out of the six boys worked for the postal service in various positions. We were a true-to-life postal family indeed. My advice to anyone, however, is to diversify. But let me continue. As postmaster I was responsible for people and things. Things I can take care of. People I cannot. You see I care too much for people. I did everything and anything for my employees. I wanted to be liked and even loved by my employees. But in order for this to happen I neglected my family. I did not have to neglect my family. I made that choice on some level. I fooled myself into thinking that if I worked hard and moved up in the ranks I would do better for my family. Wrong on so many levels.

I forgot to love my wife and children like I loved my job. Not the people so much, but the job. However, once I lost my balance, I had to turn to my wife for guidance. Guidance she always was giving, but I was not listening to. Oh, the love of a good woman. My wife is the smartest person I know and I know a lot of people.

To make a long story short, I showed my employees the attention I should have shown my wife. She said all the things a wife should say in order for her spouse to survive in this harsh world. I simply did not listen. I was foolish and proud of my male determination and false sense of self-worth.

This is where the 25 letters of Christmas came into play. One day I was thinking down on myself, than I came to the realization that these are the best of times, not the worst. I have been given a second chance to be a husband and a father. Not many get a chance at a rebirth. Right then and there I made up my mind. I was going to make the best of the situation. I was going to love my wife the way I promised her when we first met and fell in love. I demanded that I wanted that time back. I wanted her to know that I have her back and that we will fight to the end together. No job situation will come between us again. Be it boss or employee. I am the leader of my household not outside influences. Quite liberating.

Out of this clarity came the 25 letters of Christmas. I wanted her to know in no uncertain terms that I am her husband and that she is the love of my life. But more than that, we are two people joined together by God. If I am to be the priest of my household I must know God again on a personal level. I must demonstrate daily my love for Him before I can begin to love me or my wife or my children. It is a wonderful feeling to be born again. I said to myself, "I will not" let this opportunity slip through my hands this time. I will grab and hold onto it like it was my last breath.

My sweet and wonderful bride will know everyday that she is the one that I delight in and that she is the one that the Lord has blessed me to be united with. I made a vow to God, not the United States Postal Service.

To share these letters with the world is my gift to those individuals that have lost their way and need a light in order to ignite the flame back into their marriage or relationship. But, more importantly to understand that the vows you gave during your wedding day or the love declared to that special someone is not time dated, but everlasting and strong. They will get you through the hard times and will make you a king or a queen in your household. Take your rightful place. Enjoy.

Wade J. Savage

The 25 Days of Christmas

Dear Sweetheart,

Merry Christmas. This will be the best Christmas you ever had. Twenty-five days is not enough to show my love for you, but I am going to try to show you everyday with a special gift that will scream out just how beautiful you are to me.

I can never really show you the full scope of my love for you. You are my everything. I could have never made it this past year without your love and support. I know it was hard for you and I know you still have difficult days, but with your loving kindness I have found myself and I have build my faith even deeper in the Lord. I have always wanted to be the priest of my household, but I never knew how. I still have questions, but I do know that I must respect you to the fullest extent possible, just as God has loved us endlessly.

Merry Christmas, I love you and this is only day one. Enjoy.

Love,

Wade

God's love for Us

Romans 8:35-39

WHO SHALL SEPARATE us from the love of Christ? Shall tribulation, or distress, or persecution, or famine, or nakedness, or peril, or sword? Just as it is written, "For thy sake we are being put to death all day long; we were considered as sheep to be slaughtered". But in all these things we overwhelmingly conquer through Him who loved us. For I am convinced the neither death, nor life, nor angels, nor principalities, nor things present, nor things to come, nor powers, nor height, nor depth, nor any other created thing, shall be able to separate us from the love of God, which is in Christ Jesus our Lord.

Reflections: God's love for us is overwhelming. He has shown me that His relationship with his children is unlike any relationship we know here on Earth. I could never push Him away from me and nor will He ever leave me. Therefore, I must take God's example and love my wife without limitations. So understand—all commitments of love should be everlasting.

25 Days of Christmas

Merry Christmas Sweetheart,

Day 2 of my very Merry Christmas celebration of you as the love of my life. The Lord has so blessed us to be together and to have a family that we can love and grow with. I have enjoyed everyday with you. I could not have dreamed of a better life with the women that I have loved since the first day I set my eyes on her. That is you, Andrea. You are the person I want to grow old with. I pray you feel the same.

We have each other, but more importantly we have our Lord, Jesus Christ on our side. He has never forsaken us and nor will He. We have made it thus far, let's keep growing in love and respect for each other for the Lord has put us together and we will let nothing keep us apart.

Merry Christmas,

Wade

Togetherness

Ephesians 2:19-22

SO THEN YOU are no longer strangers and aliens, but you are fellow citizens with the saints, and are of God's household, having been built upon the foundation of the apostles and prophets, Christ Jesus Himself being the corner stone, in whom the whole building, being fitted together is growing into a holy temple in the Lord; in whom you also are being built together into a dwelling of God in the Spirit.

Reflections: Marriage vows are a spoken bond of togetherness. God has provided us a blueprint for togetherness. He has left us with a key to His house. His kingdom is our home for eternity and is the foundation upon which the apostles and prophets have provided us in order to enter God's home. If we listen to His instructions and provisions we will always have a home to give us comfort.

25 Days of Christmas

Merry Christmas My Love,

This is Days 3 of my love fest in celebration of our love and marriage that has been put together by God. Christmas is a time for the celebration of the birth of Jesus Christ, our Savior. In addition to Jesus' birth, I would like to celebrate the birth of our children. The Lord has truly blessed us with the most wonderful children in the world. I give you all the credit, because you have been nothing if not excellent in your care and love for our gifts from above: Cory, Christian and Cornelius.

Enjoy your day because everyday is a special day indeed.

Merry Christmas My Love,

Wade

Children

Luke 18: 15-17

AND THEY WERE bringing even their babies to Him so that He might touch them, but when the disciples saw it, they began rebuking them. But Jesus called them, saying, "Permit the children to come to Me and do not hinder them, for the kingdom of God belongs to such as these.

Reflections: Children are the wonders of God. I could not celebrate the love of my wife without celebrating my children. We as parents also have an obligation to bring our children to see the light of God. Any gift we give them cannot add up to the beautiful gift of salvation and glory.

25 Days of Christmas

Merry Christmas My Love,

This is Day 4 of my tribute to the most loving woman in my life. This is the day that the Lord has made. Let us be glad and rejoice in it. That is just what I am going to do. I am going to rejoice in the fact that I am married to the most wonderful woman in the world. You have given all you have to this marriage. You have been everything that I dreamed of from the very first time I met you playing next to my grandmother's house.

We will always have each other. We will have our Lord to guide us during the bad days, but we will have our Lord to celebrate during the good days as well. This is a great day. With you by my side, everyday is a great day.

Merry Christmas My Love

Wade

Protection, God is always with us

2 Thessalonians 3:3

B UT THE LORD is faithful, and He will strengthen and protect you from the evil one.

Reflections: Just as I am celebrating my marriage to a most beautiful woman, I am also celebrating God's power and protection over us. He guides us through the dark times by providing comfort and wisdom to us. His love is bountiful and full.

25 Days of Christmas

Merry Christmas My Darling Sweetheart,

This is Day 5 of my journey into the most beautiful trip of my life. A trip that will lead us to fortify the love we have for each. This renewal of our love will be the main reason we make our love last forever.

We make a wonderful couple. Let's not forget the vow we made to each other, "For better or for worse". This has definitely been a worse moment. But God has saw it fit to make a bad situation into a beautiful display of love and affection that hardly can be matched by many couples. We are a family; a family that understands that no one is perfect, but with each other's love and support, we can overcome many obstacles. We have overcome many trials and tribulations. Praise God because He has shown us the light of love and strength.

Merry Christmas. Andrea you are a pillar of strength and determination.

Wade

Forgiveness

1 John 1:8-9

I F WE SAY that we have no sin, we are deceiving ourselves, and the truth is not in us. If we confess our sins, He is faithful and righteous to forgive us our sins and to cleanse us from all unrighteousness.

Reflections: If you confess your sins and understand we are all sinners God will forgive you. So with Jesus' example you must forgive yourself and turn your life over to God and His son Jesus Christ. He will ease your mind and bless your soul.

25 Days of Christmas

Merry Christmas Andrea,

This is Day 6 of our 25 Days of Christmas and the love is strong and mighty. You are strong and mighty my love. You have a strong and determined mind. With all that one has to go through in life, Andrea you have shown an amazing ability to shine and grow your love every time. God has angels all around us and you my dear are most esuriently an angel from above.

We do not always know how or when we will touch people with our love and kindness, but you can be rest assured that you have more handprints than any other angel. People will not always immediately recognize the gift given them, but eventually everyone realizes the exact moment an angel came into their life. My moment was the time I saw you working at Pier One Imports on Rolling Road and I knew right there that I had made a mistake by not confusing my love for you sooner. But I remember your beautiful smile touching my heart in a way it has never been touched before or since.

I want to keep my angel happy. This is Day 6, but more importantly another day with you. The light I live I want to shine on you.

Merry Christmas My Angel of Love, Wade

Angels, Security

Philippians 4:6-7

B E ANXIOUS FOR nothing, but in everything by prayer and supplication with thanksgiving let your requests be made known to God. And the peace of God, which surpasses all comprehension, shall guard your hearts and your minds in Christ Jesus.

Reflections: Angels are here to give us a sense of comfort. When we are alone in our thoughts and no one is around, it is a blessing to know we have a friend in Jesus Christ. Angels are His representatives. Just as angels are His representatives we must take on the responsibility of caring for others.

25 Days of Christmas

Merry Christmas my Darling Sweetheart,

This is Day 7 of our Christmas Celebration. What a wonderful time it has been? Laughter and joy with our boys and happy and renewed with the ones you love. I truly believe that God has made Christmas time to be a time of renewal, a time of reflection, a time of new beginnings.

We have renewed our commitment to each other in a way that is glorious and fine. We have reflected on our past in order to understand what we must do to fortify our future. We both understand that this is a new beginning for us. We have been given a second chance to fulfill our wedding vows with earnest and zeal.

I'm happy. I'm in love with you. You make the season so bright and so meaningful for so many people. I now want to make Christmas a blessing unto you.

Merry Christmas Arnie,

Wade

Integrity must be protected, Commitment

Psalm 119:1-2

HOW BLESSED ARE those whose way is blameless, who walk in the law of the Lord. How blessed are those who observe His testimonies, who seek Him with all their heart.

Reflections: Who ever walks in the law of the Lord are both blameless and committed in the Lord. With love a commitment must be made. God has committed His love to us, therefore we must commit ourselves to the people we love. Again, we must use God as our example.

DAY 8

25 Days of Christmas

Merry Christmas Santa's Helper,

This is Day 8 of our 25-Day celebration of the birth of Jesus Christ our Lord. You make the holiday so sweet and wonderful. No matter what the circumstance, you never let it distract from the beauty of the Christmas season. I am truly blessed to have you in my life. I never could have made it without you. You are my soul provider and my heavenly blessing from high above. I don't know why He blessed me with you and I only hope that I can show you the same love and kindness that you have shown me.

When I say I have taken care of a few things, I want that to also mean that I have taken care of you by giving you all that you so desire and deserve. I want God to know that I have taken care of His angelic gift to me. Every day is a good day when I can see your smiling face in the morning. The glow of love that you emanate is wonderful indeed.

Merry Christmas Baby,

Wade

Take care of a few things, Responsibility

Matthews 25:23

"HIS MASTER SAID to him, ""Well done, good and faithful servant; you were faithful with a few things, I will put you in charge of many things; enter into the joy of your master."

Reflections: When we commit ourselves to someone we must understand we are telling God we will be faithful in our care and dedication of His creation.

25 Days of Christmas

Merry Christmas Andrea,

This is Day 9 of our 25 Days of Christmas and unfortunately you are a little under the weather. So I will keep this one short. As a matter of fact I will simply pray for you.

Dear Lord,

I come to you today, asking for a healing blessing for Andrea. Please, Lord, take away the discomfort and pain she may be feeling. Let her know that you and you alone can restore her back to her natural self. You will never forsake her or let her go. Please Lord, heal her body, heal her soul, and heal her mind. You are God and God all by yourself; therefore I come to you today asking for my dear sweetheart, Andrea, a healing. Take away her Multiple Sclerosis. Take away her stress. Give her strength and the working of her limps. Let her know that she is your child and that you will always provide for her. And Lord, forgive her of all her sins. She loves you and she knows you died on the cross in order to save her from all her sins. I thank you, Lord. Thank you for blessing my family during these difficult times. In the name of Jesus Christ I pray, Amen.

Merry Christmas Andrea,

Wade

25 Days of Christmas

Merry Christmas Baby,

This is the tenth day of our Christmas celebration and all is going strong. Our love is strong. Our faith is strong. Our family is strong. And our fellowship with the Lord is strong.

We can do no more than love Jesus. He is our salvation and glory. He died on the cross to save us from our sins. Not His sins, but our sins. What a marvelous thing indeed. That is what I want to do for you, Andrea. I want to put my faith to the test. I want you to know that I am willing to sacrifice my being in order for you to flourish. I believe in you and I will do all I can in order to see you have all the blessings you deserve. May the Lord give me the strength to carry on in His Light? He sees the burdens I have withstood and He knows my love for Him has never diminished. Pray for me as I pray for you.

Merry Christmas Baby,

Wade

Mercy, God saves us . . . He died for our sins

Titus 3:5-7

H E SAVED US, not on the basis of deeds which we have done in righteousness, but according to His mercy, by the washing of regeneration and renewing by the Holy Spirit, whom He poured out upon us richly through Jesus Christ our Savior, that being justified by His grace we might be made heirs according to the hope of eternal life.

Reflections: God simply loves us. We were made in His image. Jesus Christ died on the cross to save us from our sins, not His. Do we love without limitations? Think upon the cross and the love Christ demonstrated toward us.

25 Days of Christmas

Merry Christmas My Dear,

I have not forgotten the 11th day of Christmas. We had a busy day yesterday, a lot going on around us. Major changes are on the way. We are finally seeing the light of being right and holding onto the promises of God.

We have never wavered in our trust. You have always believed in me and I in you. We will make it. We will have our reward with our relationship with God.

Merry Christmas Andrea,

Wade

Suffering, Holding onto the promises of God

1 Peter 2:21

FOR YOU HAVE been called for the purpose, since Christ also suffered for you, leaving you an example for you to follow in His steps . . .

Reflections: We all can have a relationship with God. A tried and true relationship we can depend on. A relationship that is wonderful in its simplicity and form. All we have to do is confess our love and trust in the Lord and we will have a relationship that is build on unwavering love and devotion.

25 Days of Christmas

Merry Christmas Santa's Helper,

This is Day 12 and all is going well. We have made it this far by faith while leaning on the blessings of God.

This is my day to say thank you for being such a loving and devoted wife, mother, friend, and supporter. This family is strong because of the hard work and dedication you have put forth. I learn so much from you. However, it is now time for you to take a break and time for me to be the bulwark of the family. I will do everything in my power with the blessings of God to be the best husband, father, friend and supporter that you and the boys can have.

It is my time to step to the plate and lead. You have done more than I should have asked. Pray that I stay strong and focused. Christmas is a time of renewal and fresh beginnings. Get ready. Get set. GO!

Merry Christmas,

Wade

Marriage/Family/Children

1 Corinthians 7:14

FOR THE UNBELIEVING husband is sanctified through his wife, and the unbelieving wife is sanctified through her believing husband; for otherwise your children are unclean, but now they are holy.

Reflections: Every believing spouse needs to know that their union is not man-made, but ordained from God. We must not take lightly the responsibility we have been given as believers. As believers we trust in God's love so that we can give love and hope in return.

25 Days of Christmas

Merry Christmas Pretty Lady,

This is day 13 of our 25 days of Christmas. It's movie day. Remember we are supposed to watch a Christmas movie today. I can't wait. It is always a joy to sit next to you and enjoy the warmth of your being by my side.

This has been a wonderful Christmas season and it will only get better my dear. We are blessed indeed. God has never let us down, no matter what the situation has been. I will receive the job offer and get us back on track. But more importantly, you will have me out of the house again. Enjoy. That will be my special gift to you and the family.

Merry Christmas,

Wade

Friendship/Partner

2 Corinthians 6:14

D O NOT BE bound together with unbelievers; for what partnership has righteousness and lawlessness, or what fellowship has light with darkness.

Reflections: We must be on one accord with another. Opening a line of communications is very important for any relationship. Open communication allows a person the freedom to express their desires and wishes. Resulting in an atmosphere whereas they can explain their point of view. This further allows for a sharing of ideas. All of this can be a great benefit to any marriage. The model and facilitator of this is prayer. We must follow the divine structure of prayer. God wants to have a personal relationship with each and every one of us. Prayer is the door, all we must do is knock and He will answer.

25 Days of Christmas

Merry Christmas My Dear,

This is the 14th day of Christmas and all is well with the Lord. We have come through many a difficult day, but God has always been there for us. Earlier today you said everything changes. This is true except for God. God never changes. He is the same today as He was yesterday.

We can believe in the Lord because we are His children. We are made in His image and like any parent He loves His children no matter what the sin. We just have to repent and ask for His blessings. You have so much faith in the Lord that He has put a special blessing upon you. He has made you His ambassador here on Earth. You have such a beautiful glow that your light strengthens and frees those that are fortunate enough to be touched by it. I know I have been. Thank you, Lord. You have allowed me to be touched by your ambassador here on Earth.

Merry Christmas,

Wade

Change

Hebrews 1:10-12

AND, "THOU, LORD, in the beginning didst lay the foundation of the earth, and the heavens are the work of thy hands; they will perish, but thou remain; and they all will become old as a garment, and as a mantle thou will roll them up; as a garment they will also be changed. But thou art the same, and thy years will not come to an end."

Hebrews 13:8

Jesus Christ is the same yesterday and today, yes and forever.

Reflections: Our relationship must be build upon solid ground. It has to have an unchanging foundation made of respect, assurance, and love. There should be no reason to doubt or guess what mood or reaction will be garnered during the course of a day. A good start is to be there for your spouse. Be the rock they are longing to hold on to.

25 Days of Christmas

Merry Christmas My Love,

This is day 15 of our Christmas celebration and I could not be more pleased with the way our lives have come together. Yes, we have had rough patches, but we had them together. We overcame them together in great fashion.

I cannot quote bible verse after bible verse, but what I can do is listen to God and read His word with an earnest heart. My heart wants to be filled with His joy and love so that I can spread my love and joy to you and the children. My mission is to love you unendingly and without ceasing. You are my love and my soul mate that I have longed for since I was a little boy. We are together. We are one. We will enjoy Christmas together. I pray you have a wonderful holiday season my dear.

Merry Christmas,

Wade

Hope

Romans 15:13

NOW MAY THE God of hope fill you with all joy and peace in believing, that you may abound in hope by the power of the Holy Spirit.

Reflections: Hope is our greatest resource. No matter the circumstance and no matter the hardship we always should have hope. Hope should not be whimsical and it should not seem unsure. Be strong in the Lord and have a strong faith in the Lord. Have the hope of strong possibilities. Lean on His word and understanding. His love will not fail.

25 Days of Christmas

Merry Christmas Best Mother In The World,

This is the 16th day of Christmas and I have yet to tell you how beautiful you are to me and to everyone else around you. Andrea, you are the most beautiful woman in the world. I cannot help to think how fortunate I am to be able to see your wonderful glow everyday. Your smile is enough to get me through any day, no matter the difficultly or rain.

The outward beauty you exude is beyond approach, but more stunning than that is the bountiful glow of love and caring that you have stored inside of you. This powerful force is what makes you such a wonderful person. This is what the world sees when it sees Cory, Christian, and Cornelius. They are the true manifestation of God's gifts from you to the world. For nine months the boys were surrounded by the most special of places, your womb. Everything they are and will be is because of you. They have the loving ember of your Godly glow soaked inside of their every being.

I can only hope some of that glow rubs off onto me every time I embrace you. You are the closes representation of God that I can imagine. Thank you Lord, for an angel has appeared unto me. Her name is Andrea. I will praise You everyday for You have placed her in my midst.

Merry Christmas My Angel,

Wade

Creation

Hebrews 11:3

B Y FAITH WE understand that the worlds were prepared by the word of God, so that what is seen was not made out of things which are visible.

Reflections: God spoke the word. He created all that exist. We, however, are His most special of creations. We are made in His image. We should not take this fact lightly. We must understand that when we look in the mirror we are seeing God and all of His infinite wisdom and love. Just as you see a new born baby and we say he looks like so and so, therefore, we must on a daily basis look in the mirror and say to ourselves; I am a child of God and I shall fear no evil and I will love my fellow man.

25 Days of Christmas

Merry Christmas Arnie,

This is day 17 of our wonderful Christmas story. The number seventeen is special to me because it represents the date of your birth. January 17th. A day of love and the day in which the motivating force of love in my life began. I believe we were meant for each other in a way that very few can comprehend.

You see I am nothing without you. Yes, I could live a life without you, but I could not LIVE a LIFE without you. I was build to love you in a way that befits a queen. I am tasked with loving a woman that was made in God's image. I can no more dismiss my love for you as I could dismiss my love for God. I made a vow to God to love you for better or for worst. We have both kept our promises to each other. But, I know I can do better. I want to do better. I need to do better. I will do better. You see every moment here with you is another chance for me to get it right and to show you just how much you mean to me. I want you to feel protected. To feel loved. To feel respected and to feel like you are never alone in this world.

We celebrate Christmas in order to celebrate the birth of Jesus Christ. In His birth we are assured that we are never alone in this world. Know that is true. We are never alone and with that I am never far from you as well. I am here for you sweetheart. Merry Christmas.

Wade

Marriage—Vows

Hebrews 13: 4-6

LET MARRIAGE BE held in honor among all, and let the marriage bed be undefiled; for fornicators and adulterers God will judge. Let your character be free from the love of money. Being content with what you have for He Himself has said, "I will never desert you, nor will I ever forsake you," so that we confidently say, "The Lord is my helper, I will not be afraid. What shall man do to me?"

Reflections: An important line in this verse is the passage that states "Let your character be free from the love of money." This was a hard learned lesson for me. I never followed or loved money. I did something worse. I had the illusion that if I worked day and night this meant that I was providing for my family. I was not providing, but what I actually was doing is dividing the family unit. My family needed me, not money. My wife needed a husband to there for her. Not in spirit, but to actually be there with her and for her. My children needed to talk to me not talk about me. Don't be a ghost. Be the most. Loving you family and wife means being there to do and to see.

25 Days of Christmas

Merry Christmas Mrs. Savage

This is day 18 of our very special Christmas. I hope all is going well. You deserve to have a very, very special Christmas. You bring so much joy to everyone, therefore, it would be deserving of you to be cherished and appreciated.

Sitting here by the fireplace is so warm and cozy that it gives me a special feeling of love and strength. I can feel the welling up of love coming out of my fingers as I type my letters of love and devotion to you. Writing these letters to you is in fact your gift to me. Because of the love you show me I can therefore freely express unwavering love and support of you without reservation or lack of motivation. You are my muse. You are my inspiration for all that is beautiful and right in my life.

Merry Christmas Mrs. Savage

Love must be demonstrated

Luke 6:31-35

"AND JUST AS you want people to treat you, treat them in the same way. "And if you love those who love you, what credit is that to you?" For even sinners love those who love them. "And if you do good to those who do good to you, what credit is that to you?" For even sinners do the same. "And if you lend to those from whom you expect to receive, what credit is that to you?" Even sinners lend to sinners, in order to receive back the same amount. "But love your enemies, and do good, and lend, expecting nothing in return, and your reward will be great, and you will be sons of the Most High; for He Himself is kind to ungrateful and evil men. "Be grateful, just as your Father is merciful.

Reflections: Expecting nothing is a very difficult concept, but a very loving concept. I expect nothing from man because God has provided all for me. This is something we all need to realize. We need to realize that the people we have in our lives are blessings in many forms. These blessings may not manifest themselves in a may we completely understand, however, we must acknowledge the fact that God is our father and the He gives us gifts because He loves us and that is enough.

25 Days of Christmas

Merry Christmas My Very Special Friend,

Merry Christmas sweetheart, this is the 19th day of our celebration and what a wonderful day indeed. Everyday I wake up and get to see your lovely face is a day to celebrate. A day to say you know what? God has blessed me to an unlimited amount. I can never thank Him enough for the love He has shown.

I also thank you for being there for me this year. Rough year, but we have us. We put our trust in the Lord and He has never let us down. He has allowed us to communicate our needs and desires in a way that allows us to move forward and uplift each other in our time of despair.

I know that I have a friend that will never leave me or forsake me. That friend is you. I may not have appreciated this fact the way I should have. But, God has shown me who and what I should treasure in this world. I honor you my dear. I love you. Let's agree to love each forever. Nothing will ever separate us. Jesus Christ was born for us. He lived for us. And He died for us. So let us not let Him down. We will uphold our vows to each other because we made them to Him.

Merry Christmas My Very Special Friend,

Wade

Grace

2 Corinthians 3: 5-6

NOT THAT WE are adequate in ourselves to consider anything as coming from ourselves, but our adequacy is from God, who also made us adequate as servants of a new covenant not of the letter, but of the Spirit; for the letter kills, but the Spirit gives life.

Reflections: None of the love we give each other is from us. The love is from God. We as believers have a special gift from God, His grace.

25 Days of Christmas

Merry Christmas Andrea,

This has been a most difficult 20th day of Christmas. However, everyday is a beautiful day here on Earth when you have Jesus in your heart and on your mind. We have both going for us. Our Lord and Savior Jesus Christ has been with us every step of the way in our journey toward financial stability.

He says just ask and it shall be received. I have asked for your love and I have received it beyond measure. I have asked for a family and He has seen it fit to give me the most beautiful family in the land. I have asked for a home and He has given me a wonderful house in which we can call a home. I have asked for a career and He had given that to me as well. I now just ask for a financial blessing that will restore us back to our rightful place in His kingdom here on Earth.

I have more than the faith of a mustard seed. I have a tremendous amount of faith. My soul was rocked yesterday, but my soul is thus stronger because of His love for me and because I know I have a family that is firmly behind me no matter the twist and turns man try to throw in our way toward blessed assurance.

I (we) will remain strong.

Merry Christmas,

Wade

Faith

Luke 17:6

AND THE LORD said, "If you had faith like a mustard seed, you would say to this mulberry tree, 'Be uprooted and be planted in the sea'; and it would obey you.

Reflections: We here on Earth have concepts, calculations, and theories. We need proof. We have to touch a substance to know it is real. We have to follow a set of logical conclusions. Faith, however, is to the contrary. Faith is the power of God in its spiritual form. Faith is one's pure embodiment of love and trust in God.

25 Days of Christmas

Merry Christmas My Fine Lady,

This has been the most special of days. This is day 21 of our wonderful 25-Day celebration of Christmas. This is a special day because this is the day the Lord has made and we have been glad and we have rejoiced. It is Sunday and we have praised the Lord with both our heart and minds. But, more importantly, we have celebrated the birth of our Lord with the singing of our voices.

We left our problems at the altar. We will not want nor will we worry. The Lord is great indeed and as the song goes, "He is mighty; He is mighty; He is mighty indeed." God will provide for us, all we have to do is honor Him with our love and devotion. We do love Him and we do honor Him.

Merry Christmas, Andrea

Wade

Prayer, Exaltation

Luke 1:46-50

AND MARY SAID: "My soul exalts the Lord, and my spirit has rejoiced in God my Savior, for He has had regard for the humble state of His bond slave; For behold, from this time on all generations will count me blessed. For the Mighty One has done great things for me; and holy is His name. And His mercy is upon generation after generation toward those who fear Him.

Reflections: We must go to the alter everyday and praise God for His marvelous wonders. When we sing we should have praise on our heart and God on our mind.

25 Days of Christmas

Merry Christmas Pretty Lady,

This is day 22 of our joyous celebration of Christmas. When I first started this 25-day love letter to you in honor our Lord Jesus Christ, I did not know it would be such a blessing to our marriage.

It seems like we talk everyday now about our love for each other. Saying things we always wanted to say to each other, but never had the time or words to say. 2008 has been a most difficult year for us, but the Lord has seen us out of the fire and into the wonderful light of His grace and mercy. I would not trade 2008 for anything in the world because if nothing else it has taught me that nothing, NOTHING, is greater than you and the boys. No job. No friend. No project. NOTHING. I must always keep my eye on the prize. That prize is the love of God and the keeping of my vows to you and the boys.

Merry Christmas Pretty Lady,

Wade

God's Word

2 Peter 1: 2-7

GRACE AND PEACE be multiplied to you in the knowledge of God and of Jesus our Lord; seeing that His divine power had granted to us everything pertaining to life and godliness, through the true knowledge of Him who called us by His own glory and excellence. For by these He has granted to us His precious and magnificent promises, in order that by them you might become partakers of the divine mature, having escaped the corruption that is in the world by lust. Now for this very reason also, applying all diligence, in your faith supply moral excellence, and in your moral excellence knowledge; and in your knowledge, self-control, and in your self-control, perseverance, and in your perseverance, godliness; and in your godliness, brotherly kindness, and in your brotherly kindness, love.

Reflections: Coming to knowledge always involves an orderly process. The knowledge of God's word is no different. We all reach our divine maturity in proper order and respect. The order of knowledge in God's word is diligence, faith, self-control, perseverance, godliness, brotherly kindness, and love.

25 Days of Christmas

Merry Christmas my One and Only,

We have two days left before Christmas Day and I am so excited. I am excited because I can truly say that I will be home for Christmas enjoying my wife and children as we go through the day with tithing and great joy.

Christmas is a time for family and friends. We will make the best of our circumstance because we know Jesus is our best friend and the head of our family. We may never fully understand His plan for us, but we do know that His plan is perfect.

I am excited to be here, living for our Lord. We will rejoice and be glad in it.

Merry Christmas Baby,

Wade

Unity

Colossians 3: 14-17

AND BEYOND ALL these things put on love, which is the perfect bond of unity. And let the peace of Christ rule in your hearts, to which indeed you were called in one body; and be thankful. Let the word of Christ richly dwell within you, with all wisdom teaching and admonishing one another with psalms and hymns and spiritual songs, singing with thankfulness in your hearts to God. And whatever you do in word or deed, do all in the name of the Lord Jesus, giving thanks through Him to God the Father.

Reflections: We are "one body". The word of Christ must dwell in us all. The only true measure of giving thanks to our Lord Jesus Christ is to act on one accord. Showing love toward your fellow man is the single most uplifting act any of us could commit. Where there are two or three gathered let there be praise in the air. Sing to the full measure of your soul and devotion to our Lord and Savior, Jesus Christ.

25 Days of Christmas

Merry Christmas,

It was the night before Christmas, and all through the house, not a creature was stirring, not even a mouse. You know the rest. It is day 24 of our 25 days of Christmas, Sweetheart. We have a busy day ahead of us. But remember it is us; we are not alone. I will be there for you forever.

This has been the best Christmas ever for me. I think it is because I have fully focused my attention on you and the boys and not on work. God saw it fit to be so. I will not doubt.

I love you. Merry Christmas.

Wade

God is Good

1 Timothy 4: 4-5

FOR EVERYTHING CREATED by God is good, and nothing is to be rejected, if it is received with gratitude; for it is sanctified by means of the word of God and prayer.

Reflections: In the beginning, God created the heavens and the earth. And God created man in His own image, in the image of God He created him, male and female, He created them. Every creation by God is good. This also refers to our circumstances. We as a couple have taken the situation we were in and trusted on the Lord for guidance and protection. We never cursed God. Instead, we have prayed to God and we have thanked Him for His blessings. We have trusted the word of God and He has blessed us for our faith in His word.

25 Days of Christmas

Merry Christmas Andrea,

It is Christmas morning and the family is together. That is the most special of all the gifts here today. We have each other and we need each other. Andrea, you are the glue that keeps us together. I must now remember that you need me to keep us together, as husband and wife. I am there for you as you are there for me.

Let us celebrate the birth of Jesus Christ our Lord and Savior. Merry Christmas and may you have a Happy New Year.

Wade

Jesus Christ

1 John 4: 9-16

BY THIS, THE love of God was manifested in us; that God has sent His only begotten Son into the world so that we might live through Him. In this is love, not that we loved God, but that He loved us and sent His Son to be the propitiation for our sins. Beloved, if God so loved us, we also ought to love one another. No one has beheld God at any time; if we love one another, God abides in us, and His love is perfected in us. By this we know that we abide in Him and He in us, because He has given us of His Spirit. And we have beheld and bear witness that the Father has sent the Son to be the Savior of the world. Whoever confesses that Jesus is the Son of God, God abides in him, and he in God. And we have come to know and have believed the love, which God has for us. God is love, and the one who abides in love abides in God, and God abides in him.

Reflections: God sent His Son to show mankind what love is supposed to be. Jesus Christ is our Savior. We must just confess that Jesus is the Son of God, live in His word and love Him unconditionally. I have learned to trust Him without waiver. I have been put to the test like Job. I have come through the fire and I am pleased because my life is richer with joy and happiness. I have trusted God with my life and He has rewarded me with His blessings.

Made in the USA
Middletown, DE
02 December 2020